D0163996

SHAREHOLDER YIELD

A Better Approach to

Dividend Investing

Mebane T. Faber

Acknowledgements

Most financial writing owes a major debt of gratitude to the research that has come before it. In this case there have been many analysts and researchers that have examined the effects of selecting stocks based on various measures of cash flows and their distributions. While we mention a number of these pioneers in this piece, we would especially like to acknowledge William Priest, James O'Shaughnessy, Patrick O'Shaughnessy, Jacob Boudoukh, Roni Michaely, Matthew Richardson, Eugene Fama, Kenneth French, Michael Roberts, Michael Maubossin, Richard Tortoriello, Rob Arnott, Jason Hsu, Robert Haugen, Jeremy Schwartz, Wes Gray, Jack Vogel, and Daniel Peris for their fine work.

To Mom, Dad, and my big brothers.

Contents

Introduction

"The Blind Men and the Elephant"

It was six men of Indostan
To learning much inclined,
Who went to see the Elephant
(Though all of them were blind),
That each by observation
Might satisfy his mind.

The *First* approach'd the Elephant,
And happening to fall
Against his broad and sturdy side,
At once began to bawl:
"God bless me! but the Elephant
Is very like a wall!"

The *Second*, feeling of the tusk,
Cried, -"Ho! what have we here
So very round and smooth and sharp?
To me 'tis mighty clear
This wonder of an Elephant
Is very like a spear!"

The *Third* approached the animal,

And happening to take

The squirming trunk within his hands,

Thus boldly up and spake:

"I see," quoth he, "the Elephant

Is very like a snake!"

The *Fourth* reached out his eager hand,

And felt about the knee.

"What most this wondrous beast is like

Is mighty plain," quoth he,

"'Tis clear enough the Elephant

Is very like a tree!"

The *Fifth*, who chanced to touch the ear,

Said: "E'en the blindest man

Can tell what this resembles most;

Deny the fact who can,

This marvel of an Elephant

Is very like a fan!"

The *Sixth* no sooner had begun

About the beast to grope,

Then, seizing on the swinging tail

That fell within his scope,

"I see," quoth he, "the Elephant

Is very like a rope!"

And so these men of Indostan

Disputed loud and long,

Each in his own opinion

Exceeding stiff and strong,

Though each was partly in the right,

And all were in the wrong!

MORAL.

So oft in theologic wars,

The disputants, I ween,

Rail on in utter ignorance

Of what each other mean,

And prate about an Elephant

Not one of them has seen!

John Godfrey Saxe's (1816-1887) version of the famous Indian legend.

This parable originated in India, and while different versions exist in various Buddhist, Hindu, and modern traditions, the general story remains the same. Each blind man touches a different part of the elephant and, when asked to describe what he feels, comes up with a different response. In the end, the king conveys the moral that, while each opinion may represent a piece of the truth, in isolation from one another, no single perspective reveals the whole story.

What does this have to do with investing? In many cases, whether evaluating a stock or some macro influence on the economy, we must be diligent in seeking out other perspectives and consistently question what it is we are "seeing." Often, only after the fact (and after much devastation to the value of a portfolio), do we realize that we only saw a small piece of the overall picture.

Most research analysts focus on the operations of a company. While operations are certainly important, the role of capital allocation in the future success of the company is often overlooked. A recent book that Warren Buffett recommended examines this understudied topic - *The Outsiders: Eight Unconventional CEOs and Their Radically Rational Blueprint for Success* by Thorndike. A quote from the book:

> "CEOs need to do two things well to be successful: run their operations efficiently and deploy the cash generated by those operations. Most CEOs (and the management books they write or read) focus on managing operations, which is undeniably important.
>
> Basically CEOs have five essential choices for deploying capital – investing in existing operations, acquiring other businesses, paying down debt, or repurchasing stock – and three alternatives for raising it – tapping internal cash flow, issuing debt, or raising equity. Think of these options collectively as a tool kit. Over the long term, returns for shareholders will be determined largely by the decisions a CEO makes in choosing which tools to use (and which to avoid) among these various options….In fact, this role just might be the most important responsibility any CEO has, and yet despite its importance, there are no courses in capital allocation at the top business schools.

This short research piece exposes the reader to certain presuppositions about investing, as well as examines overlooked capital allocation decisions that deserve closer attention. We take a look at the various ways in which a company uses its cash flow and the resulting impact on its stock, and ponder the question with respect to dividends, "Is this the whole picture, or am I only holding the elephant's trunk?"

CHAPTER 1

Dividend Investing Works

Well Over Time

Dividends and their reinvestment represent a major portion of a stock investor's total return over time. Examination of equity returns back to 1871 in the United States dramatically illustrates this property. An investor in US stocks would have realized an 8.83% compound return from 1871 -2011. However, excluding dividends and their reinvestment would have reduced the portfolio's compound return to 4.13% a year, demonstrating that reinvested dividends represent over half of an investor's annualized returns over the period. While most investors focus myopically on stock price gyrations, dividends have proven to be the slow, but steady engine that drives returns over time.

Analyzing the final value of a portfolio invested in US stocks since 1871 reinforces this view. Figure 1 demonstrates that, if one had invested $100 in 1871 in the price return index, by the end of 2011, it would have compounded to $28,887 (gross of fees, transaction costs, and taxes). When we consider the total return portfolio, which reflects price return and dividend reinvestment, the ending value jumps to $13,955,952, a 480-fold improvement!

By reinvesting dividends and compounding the portfolio returns, the final value of the total return portfolio turns out to be 99.8% higher than the non-dividend portfolio. This suggests that over long periods, dividends contribute virtually all of the final portfolio value versus a price only return. (To be fair, if companies didn't pay out cash dividends then the result would be the portfolio gains coming from price appreciation, but that is a hypothetical scenario.)

FIGURE 1 – US Stocks, Total Return vs. Price Return, 1871-2011.

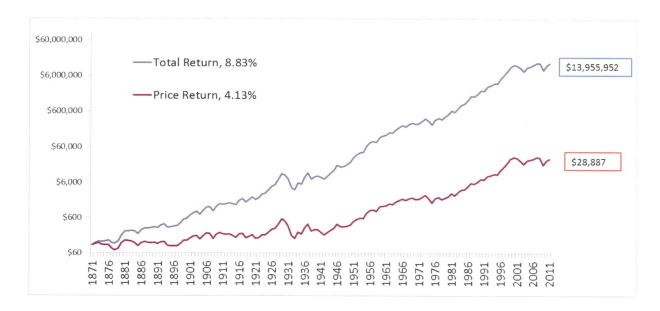

Source: Shiller. Data before 1926 are based on Cowles "Common Stock Indexes". Index returns are for illustrative purposes only. Indices are unmanaged and an investor cannot invest directly in an index. Past performance is no guarantee of future results.

While dividends have historically proven to be a major factor in determining a portfolio's final value over time, in the short term, price movements dominate the volatility of the returns. Large swings in prices have had an enormous impact on returns for time frames that range from one year to an entire decade. Figure 2, below, shows price returns (red lines) and the dividend yield (blue line) by year since 1871, and the variability of the price returns swamps the steady dividend yield returns.

FIGURE 2 – US Stocks, Dividend Returns vs. Price Returns, 1871-2011.

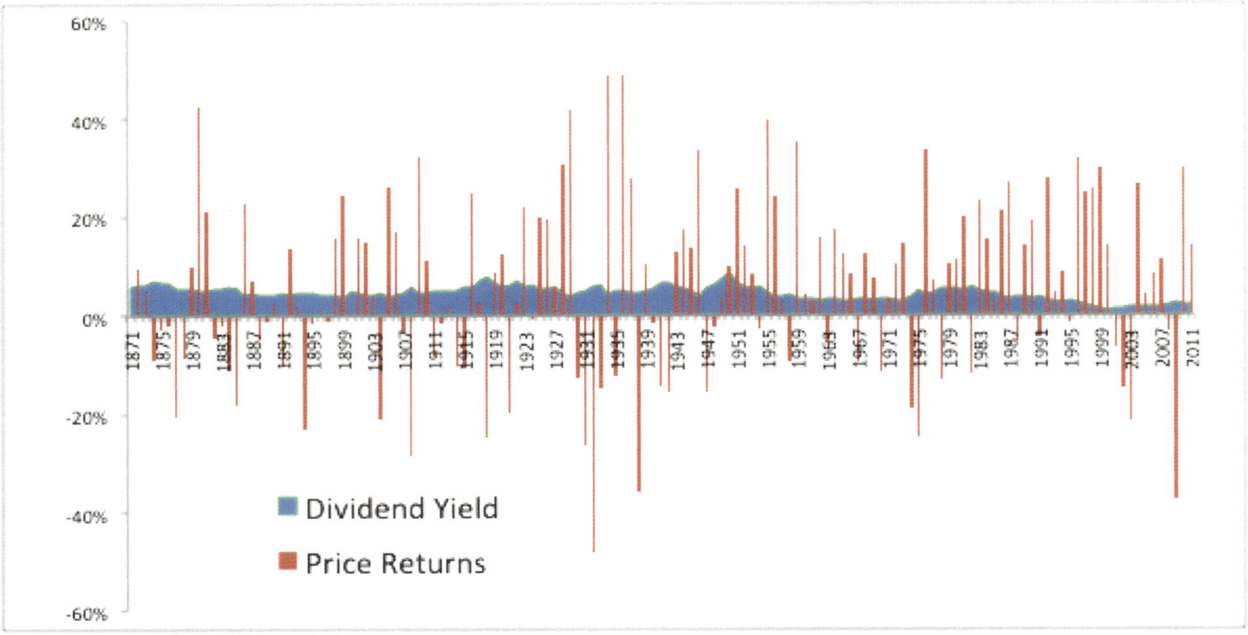

Source: Shiller. Data before 1926 are based on Cowles "Common Stock Indexes". Index returns are for illustrative purposes only. Indices are unmanaged and an investor cannot invest directly in an index. Past performance is no guarantee of future results.

In Figure 3 below, it is clear that, even at the decade time frame, price movements have a major impact on total returns. Price-to-earnings (P/E) ratio expansion (i.e. price increases) had a major positive impact on total returns in the 1920s and 1990s, while the reverse occurred in the 1930s and 2000s. Even the steady contribution of dividends could not prevent the equity markets from experiencing negative total returns in the 1930s and 2000s.

FIGURE 3 – S&P 500 Dividend Return and Price Return by Decade, 1871-2010.

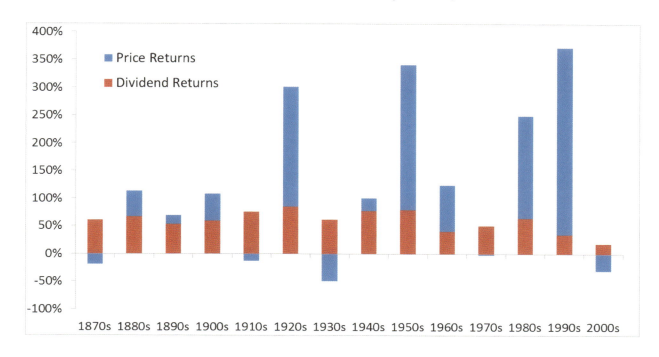

Source: Shiller, Author, Data before 1926 are based on Cowles "Common Stock Indexes". Index returns are for illustrative purposes only. Indices are unmanaged and an investor cannot invest directly in an index. Past performance is no guarantee of future results.

This major contribution of dividends to total return is even more apparent when valuation is taken into account.

Benjamin Graham and David Dodd are universally seen as the fathers of valuation and security analysis. In their 1934 book *Security Analysis* they were early pioneers in comparing stock prices with earnings smoothed across multiple years, preferably five to ten years. This long-term perspective allows the analyst to smooth out the business and economic cycle, as well as price fluctuations.

Robert Shiller, the author and Yale professor, popularized Graham and Dodd's methods with his version of this cyclically adjusted price-to-earnings ratio (CAPE). His 1998 paper "Valuation Ratios and the Long-Run Stock Market Outlook" was shortly followed by his book *Irrational*

Exuberance that included a warning on the overvaluation of US equities prior to the 2000 stock market crash.

Figure 4 below is a chart of the CAPE going back to 1881. The long-term series spends about half of the time with values ranging between 10 and 20, with an average and median value of about 17 (red line). The all-time low reading was 5, reached at the end of 1920, and the high value of 45 was reached at, you guessed it, the end of 1999.

FIGURE 4 – US Stocks, 10-Year CAPE, 1881-2011.

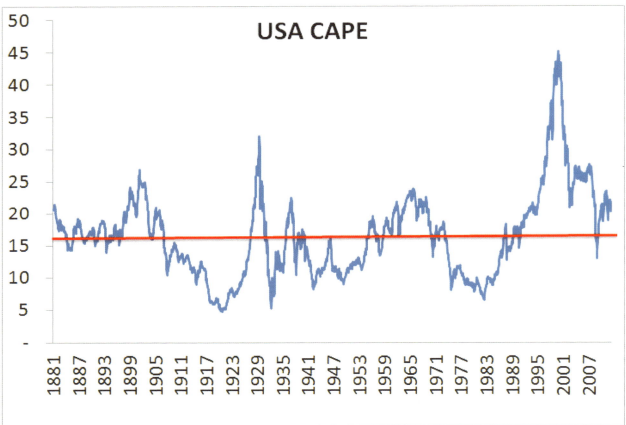

Source: Shiller. Author, Data before 1926 are based on Cowles "Common Stock Indexes". Index returns are for illustrative purposes only. Indices are unmanaged and an investor cannot invest directly in an index. Past performance is no guarantee of future results.

In Figure 5, we examine a table of all of the CAPE yearly readings at the end of the year from 1881 – 2001, and the subsequent ten-year compound real return. Not surprisingly, the lower the valuation the higher the future returns, and vice versa. When valuations are low investors have a tailwind of potential P/E multiple expansion (as markets increase in price), and likewise, a headwind when markets are expensive.

The average real return (after inflation) over the period was about 6%, but periods of extreme over- and undervaluation varied wildly from that figure. The red bar in Figure 5 is where we find ourselves at the end of 2012, at a historically high 21.

FIGURE 5 – US Stocks 10-Year Compound Returns vs. 10-Year CAPE, 1881-2011.

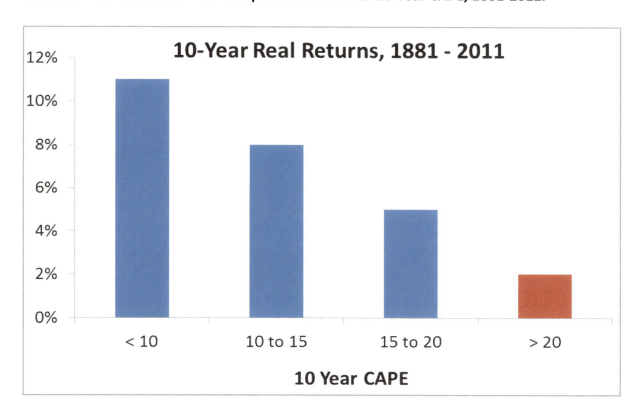

Source: Shiller. Author, Data before 1926 are based on Cowles "Common Stock Indexes". Index returns are for illustrative purposes only. Indices are unmanaged and an investor cannot invest directly in an index. Past performance is no guarantee of future results.

Also of note is that during periods of overvaluation (like now), the returns from dividends become even more critical. Figure 6 below shows the contribution of dividends to the total returns of stocks when the market is above the average valuation of 17, and also when below.

Price contributes nicely to total returns when stocks are undervalued, but it is actually a headwind and contributes negative returns when stocks are overvalued. Dividends provide all of the returns to stocks in bubbly environments!

FIGURE 6 – Dividend and Price Contribution to Total Real Returns vs. 10-Year CAPE, 1881-2011.

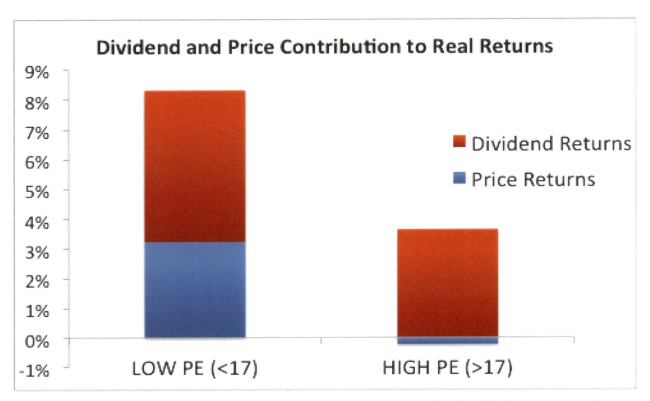

Source: Shiller. Author, Data before 1926 are based on Cowles "Common Stock Indexes". Index returns are for illustrative purposes only. Indices are unmanaged and an investor cannot invest directly in an index. Past performance is no guarantee of future results.

For those wanting to dive deeper into the macro valuation topic, our paper "Global Value: Building Trading Models with the 10 Year CAPE" goes into much greater detail as well as examining the valuation metric across approximately forty foreign equity markets.

CHAPTER 2

Dividend Yields on Stocks

While it is evident that dividends contribute a major portion of returns to an entire stock market over time, research below also indicates that higher yielding dividend stocks have performed better than stocks with little to no yield. A good summary of the dividend literature can be found in the Tweedy Browne paper entitled, "The High Dividend Return Advantage." While this study merits greater attention, we focus on a few of the highlights, below.

The finance professor, Kenneth French of Dartmouth, ranked US stocks from 1927-2010 into high, medium, low, and zero yield portfolios. He found that portfolios of stocks with the highest dividend yields returned 11.2%, stocks with low dividend yields returned 9.1%, and stocks paying no dividends returned 8.4% per year. (*2011 Global Investment Returns Yearbook.*)

Elroy Dimson, Paul Marsh and Mike Staunton completed an even longer study. They sorted the 100 largest UK stocks from 1900-2010 into high and low yield portfolios, and found that the compound returns were 10.9% and 8.0% per year, respectively.

They further corroborated these findings when they examined 21 separate countries from the more recent 1975-2010 period and found, again, that higher dividend yielding stocks outperformed low dividend yielders in every country except one (New Zealand, which only included 20 stocks). Across all countries, the dividend premium was an average of 4.4 percentage points a year. The results were even more pronounced in the high valuation environment we have been in since 2000, where high dividend yielding stocks outperformed by 9.1 percentage points on average per year. (*2011 Global Investment Returns Yearbook.*)

Interestingly enough, ranking the universe of countries by dividend yield also resulted in outperformance, a finding which was supported by a 1991 study by Michael Keppler titled, "The Importance of Dividend Yields in Country Selection." He found that the highest yielding countries outperformed the lowest yielding from 1969-1989 by more than 12 percentage points per year.

Running a similar study using a different database (Global Financial Data), we sorted countries by quartiles from 1920-2011, beginning with nine countries and expanding to eighteen by study end. We found that countries in the highest dividend paying quartile outperformed the countries in the lowest paying quartile by 11 percentage points per year.

CHAPTER 3

Dividends are Only Part of the Picture

Now that we have impressed upon you the long term evidence that investing in dividend paying stocks has led to outperformance, we want to shift gears and caution you to not just consider dividends in isolation, contently believing the elephant to be shaped like a rope.

One of the most important qualities of a successful investment analyst is the ability to adapt to change. Far too many investors adhere to their approach with a religious-like zeal, whether it is value investing, trendfollowing, modern portfolio theory, or trading based on the lunar cycle. For those investors who are proponents of investing in dividend stocks, we ask you to keep an open mind.

It is very important to be cognizant of structural changes in markets. While there are some truths that seem to be inherent to the nature of the market (highly volatile, large outliers, bubbles, booms and crashes), others truths change based on government policy, as well as macro factors.

One structural change in the stock market is that companies currently pay out a lower percentage of their earnings in cash dividends than they have in the past. As seen in Figure 7, while companies have historically paid out, on average, 60% of their earnings as dividends, this figure has been declining consistently for the past seventy years.

FIGURE 7 – S&P 500, Dividend Payout Ratio per Decade, 1880-2010.

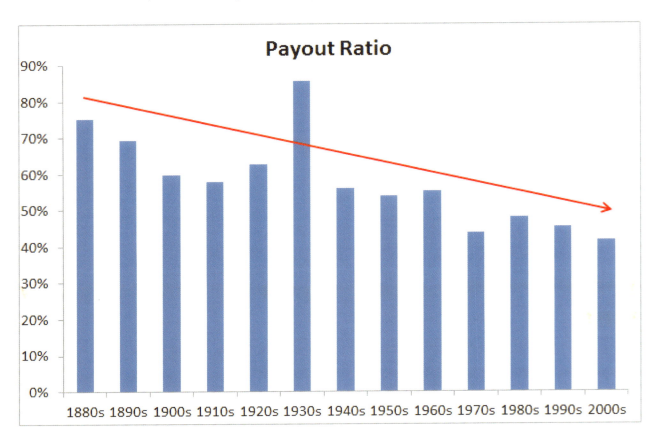

This trend has resulted in the dividend yield on stocks declining to all-time lows levels in the past decade as seen in Figure 8. The red line represents the average yield over the period of approximately 4.5%.

FIGURE 8 – S&P 500 Dividend Yield, 1871-2011.

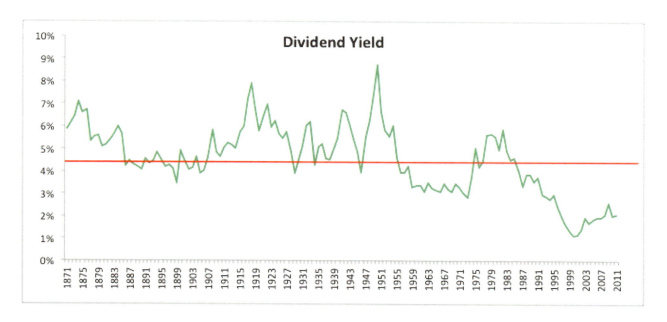

Source: Shiller. Data before 1926 are based on Cowles "Common Stock Indexes". Index returns are for illustrative purposes only. Indices are unmanaged and an investor cannot invest directly in an index. Past performance is no guarantee of future results.

When examining any fundamental shift in markets, we must analyze why the change occurred. Why are companies paying out less in cash dividends?

One of the reasons that companies pay out less in dividends is due to the SEC instituting rule 10b-18 in 1982, which provided safe harbor for firms conducting repurchases from stock manipulation charges. A noteworthy paper on trends in corporate payout policy is "Dividends, Share Repurchases, and the Substitution Hypothesis" (2002) by Grullon and Michaely. Once the government made it easier for companies to buy back their own stock, Figure 9, below, details how stock buybacks went from nearly nothing to either equaling or surpassing cash that was paid out as dividends in the late 1990s.

FIGURE 9 – US Stocks, Dividends and Buybacks, 1972 -2011.

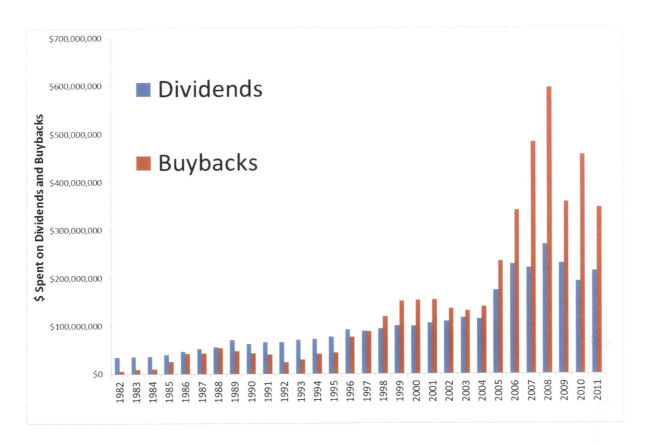

Source: Gray.

Beginning in the late 1990's share buybacks have outpaced dividend payments. Why might companies choose to buyback stock rather than payout cash dividends? Hypothetically, investors shouldn't care whether their returns come from dividends or capital gains (the so-called Modigliani-Miller theorem). This approach assumes a tax-neutral investor when, in reality, most investors are highly sensitive to tax treatment. While tax rates fluctuate with the political seasons, it has often been the case that dividends taxed as ordinary income have had inferior tax treatment to long-term capital gains that historically carry lower rates.

In over half of the past forty years, dividends have been taxed at higher rates than long-term capital gains, with the exception of 1988-1997, and 2003-present. While this disadvantage was improved by the recent Bush tax cuts and 2013 update, and while there are some foreign countries that do not have inferior tax treatment for dividends (see Appendix B for dividend and tax rates by year), the number of companies paying dividends has, nonetheless, declined from nearly 100% to around 75% for the S&P 500 companies in the U.S., and down to less than 30% for the NASDAQ Composite. (Another concise summary of dividend paying stocks is the 2001 French Fama paper "Disappearing Dividends: Changing Firm Characteristics or Lower Propensity to Pay?")

FIGURE 10 – Percentage of Companies Paying Dividends, S&P 500.

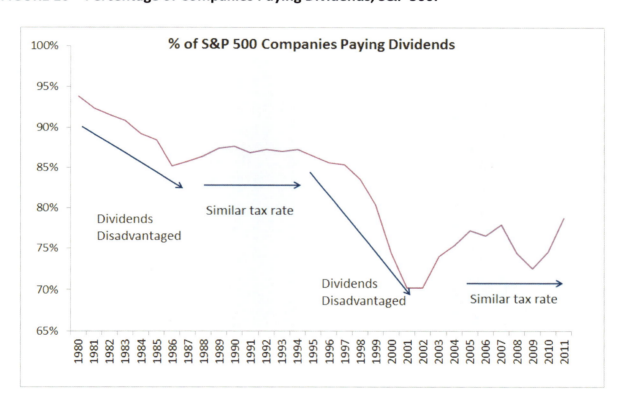

Source: Standard and Poor's, Political Calculations blog.

A recent paper by Jacob and Jacob (2011), "Taxation, Dividends and Share Repurchases: Taking Evidence Global," examines 6,416 companies across 25 countries and find that relative tax rates are hugely important. They state, "Our results show that dividend and shareholder taxation are important determinants of corporate payout internationally in the past 20 years. In countries and years in which dividends are taxed favorably relative to capital gains, firms are more likely to pay dividends, and the amount of dividends is greater. Conversely, in countries and years in which capital gains receive preferential tax treatment over dividends, firms are more likely to repurchase shares to pay out cash to investors."

Jeremy Schwartz from WisdomTree has authored some great pieces on dividends and buybacks including "The Importance of Dividends and Buybacks Ratios for Gauging Equity Values" and "When Will Apple and Google Start Paying Dividends". In the latter article he demonstrates that in 2010, companies in seven out of ten sectors bought back more stock than they paid out in cash dividends – the exceptions being materials, utilities, and telecom services.

FIGURE 11 – Sector Dividend and Buybacks as a Percentage of Total.

	% Paid in Dividends	% Paid in Buybacks
InformationTechnology	20%	80%
Consumer Discretionary	22%	78%
Health Care	35%	65%
Energy	39%	61%
Financials	39%	61%
Materials	41%	59%
Industrials	44%	56%
Utilities	54%	46%
Consumer Staples	85%	15%
Telecommunication Services	96%	4%

Source: WisdomTree, February 2012.

Once you examine the combination of dividends and net buybacks, then the picture shifts significantly.   Rather than paying out any less in aggregate cash flows to their shareholders, companies have instead changed the distribution method to reward their investors with a more favorable tax treatment. Below in Figure 12 we show the dividend yield on stocks for the past forty years as well as the net payout yield (which we touch on later but is simply dividends + stock buybacks – stock issuances).

FIGURE 12 – US Stocks, Dividend Yield vs. Dividend + Buyback Yield, 1982 – 2011.

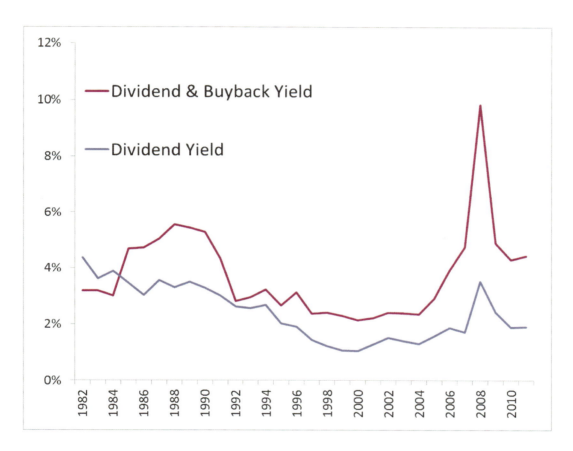

Source: Standard and Poor's.

Now that we have detailed the decline in prominence of cash dividends as a method of returning cash to shareholders, below we will examine how this shift has impacted returns to portfolios of stocks with high dividend yields, as well as portfolios based on other measures of how companies distribute their cash flows.

CHAPTER 4

Shareholder Yield

The most holistic way to approach the topic of yield investing is to examine all of the various ways in which companies distribute cash to shareholders. Companies can use their cash flow to reinvest in the business (which includes capital expenditures, research and development, and mergers and acquisitions), or, when facing difficulty achieving high rates of return on their capital, these companies can return cash to shareholders via cash dividends, debt paydown, or stock buybacks. Indeed, in the recent article by Michael Mauboussin, "Share Repurchase From All Angles," he states:

> "The purpose of a company is to maximize long-term value. As such, the prime responsibility of a management team is to invest financial, physical, and human capital at a rate in excess of the opportunity cost of capital. Operationally, this means identifying and executing strategies that deliver excess returns. Outstanding executives assess the attractiveness of various alternatives and deploy capital to where its value is highest. This not only captures investments including capital expenditures, working capital, and acquisitions, but also share buybacks. There are cases where buying back shares provides more value to continuing shareholders than investing in the business does. Astute capital allocators understand this."

The question remains: does including this additional data on alternate uses of corporate cash flows improve the ability to forecast investment returns in equities? There has been ample research that answers this question in the affirmative, and we include a brief literature review in the Appendix A. We further provide our own research below, which validates the conclusions of the research completed to date.

Below we examine stocks in the S&P 500 from 1982-2011, the period in which buybacks became more relevant with the passage of the new SEC rules. We will first examine each metric of yield – dividend yield, net buyback yield and net debt reduction yield -- in isolation before examining them in combination. (For research that details longer time frames all the way back to the 1920s, please consult the Appendix.) Since various researchers have different conceptions of yield measurement, an investor must be careful to maintain a consistent definition. We define a few different cash flow metrics and methods of cash distribution in order to discuss the research on an apples-to-apples basis.

Dividend Yield = Trailing 12 months cash dividends / market capitalization.
(Basically this means the total value of cash dividends the company paid out divided by the market value of the stock.)

Net Buyback Yield = (Trailing 12 month stock repurchases – stock issuances) / market capitalization.
(Basically this means the total value of stock buybacks divided by the market value of the stock.)

Net Payout Yield = Dividend Yield + Net Buyback Yield.
(Basically this is the combination of the two above.)

Net Debt Paydown Yield = Net changes in short and long term borrowing and debt / market capitalization.
(Basically this means the total value debt a company has paid down divided by the market value of the stock.)

Shareholder Yield = Dividend Yield + Net Buyback Yield + Net Debt Paydown Yield.

Below is a table of summary risk and the return statistics for the S&P 500 and portfolios divided into quartiles based on dividend yield, value-weighted, and rebalanced yearly. Quartiles divide the universe into four buckets where 25% of the universe, or 125 companies, fall into each bucket. Value-weighting (also known as market capitalization weighting), can result in more conservative returns to a portfolio than equal weighting but also more conservative trading assumptions for very large portfolios.

A simple method of investing in the highest yielding dividend stocks outperforms the S&P 500 by over two percentage points a year, consistent with most academic research. Volatility is in line with the broad market although drawdowns are higher, likely reflecting the increased risk to companies with higher, and possibly unsustainable, dividend payments. (Drawdown is measured as the maximum peak-to-trough loss in the portfolio on a monthly basis.) Many investors can recall this property of high yielding dividend stocks as recently as the 2008-2009 crises with many financials having seemingly high yields that were in fact not sustainable.

FIGURE 13 – Dividend Yield, 1982-2011.

	S&P 500	Lowest Yield (Q1)	Highest Yield (Q4)
Return	10.96%	9.42%	13.40%
Volatility	15.57%	19.71%	15.12%
Sharpe Ratio	0.40	0.24	0.58
Max Drawdown	-50.95%	-60.17%	-61.36%

Source: Gray, Vogel, "Enhancing the Investment Performance of Yield-Based Strategies" (2012) Index returns are for illustrative purposes only. Indices are unmanaged and an investor cannot invest directly in an index. Past performance is no guarantee of future results. Index returns do not reflect any management fees, transaction costs or expenses. This example is purely hypothetical.

In evaluating stock repurchases and debt reduction measures, it is important to use *net buyback and paydown statistics* to account for companies that are issuing lots of shares or debt at the same time that they are buying back stock and paying down other debt. Otherwise, one risks overvaluing those companies that simply buyback stock with one hand, but issue it to management with the other hand through executive stock option packages.

Dividend policy tends to be consistent, and management is often very reluctant to cut a dividend. Repurchases, as well as mergers and acquisitions, on the other hand tend to be volatile and often follow the business cycle as well as the stock market – often to the detriment of shareholders. This trend is noticeable in Figure 9 with the buyback peaks in 2000 and 2007. Since companies are more likely to spend cash when they have extra sitting around, this generally leads to more mergers and acquisitions when times are good – often right before markets turn down again. The yearly volatility from 1982-2011 of changes in dividends (7%) and capital expenditures (11%) is far less than the volatility of buybacks (49%) and mergers and acquisitions (65%).

However, in times when the underlying stock trades at a discount to intrinsic value, buybacks are a favorable use of cash. As Warren Buffett penned in a 1984 essay, "When companies with outstanding businesses and comfortable financial positions find their shares selling far below intrinsic value in the marketplace, no alternative action can benefit shareholders as surely as repurchases." Warren's partner Charlie Munger is also a fan of buybacks, and in his typical witty fashion advises investors to "look for the cannibals".

This is an interesting point that is often missed. The main reason to own a stock is that you believe it is trading at a discount to intrinsic value, in which case you want companies buying back their stock as it is a transfer of wealth from the seller to the buyer. This can be seen as a form of "value arbitrage", where the investor is looking for cheap companies that are buying back their stock. It is only in the instances when a stock is trading at a premium to intrinsic value when buybacks are value-destroying – but why would an investor ever intentionally own a stock trading above intrinsic value?

Below in Figure 14 we show that purchasing companies with high net stock buybacks resulted in roughly the same risk and returns as buying high yielding dividend stocks.

FIGURE 14 – Net Buyback Yield, 1982-2011.

	S&P 500	Lowest Yield (Q1)	Highest Yield (Q4)
Return	10.96%	9.62%	13.19%
Volatility	15.57%	18.26%	16.00%
Sharpe Ratio	0.40	0.27	0.53
Max Drawdown	-50.95%	-63.55%	-52.21%

Source: Gray, Vogel, "Enhancing the Investment Performance of Yield-Based Strategies" (2012). Index returns are for illustrative purposes only. Indices are unmanaged and an investor cannot invest directly in an index. Past performance is no guarantee of future results. Index returns do not reflect any management fees, transaction costs or expenses. This example is purely hypothetical.

Below is a visual representation of stocks in the S&P 500 as of April 2013, and how their yields compare when combining both dividends and buybacks. The portfolios are market capitalization weighted.

FIGURE 15– Various Yields, April 2013.

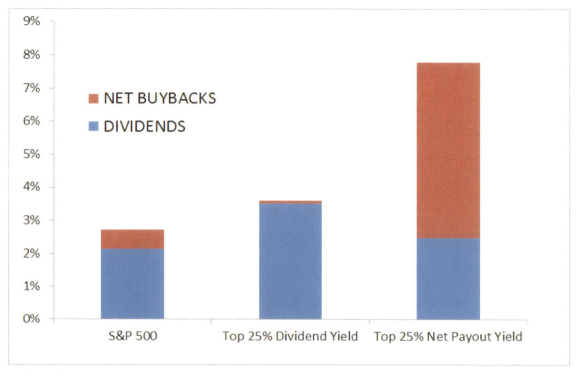

Source: Bloomberg

The dividend yield portfolio has a respectable 3.6% net payout yield, which is about 1 percentage point better than the 2.7% total net payout yield for the S&P 500. However the top net payout yield portfolio yields 7.8%. It is apparent that the combination of the two measures produces a net payout yield that is more than double that of either the S&P500 or the high dividend yield portfolio.

Below is a chart of all of the companies in the S&P 500, and as you can see most have a positive net payout yield, which is a good thing. You want to avoid the bottom 20% as they are diluting shareholders. (The bottom ten worst offenders were excluded so that the chart would still be readable.) Interestingly enough, half of the 95 companies with a negative payout yield actually had a positive dividend, including twelve companies with a dividend yield over 3%. This demonstrates why it is so important to look at all of the ways companies use their cash, as you may think you have a good dividend paying stock when in reality the company is diluting your ownership by issuing new shares (often to management).

FIGURE 16 – Net Payout Yield, April 2013.

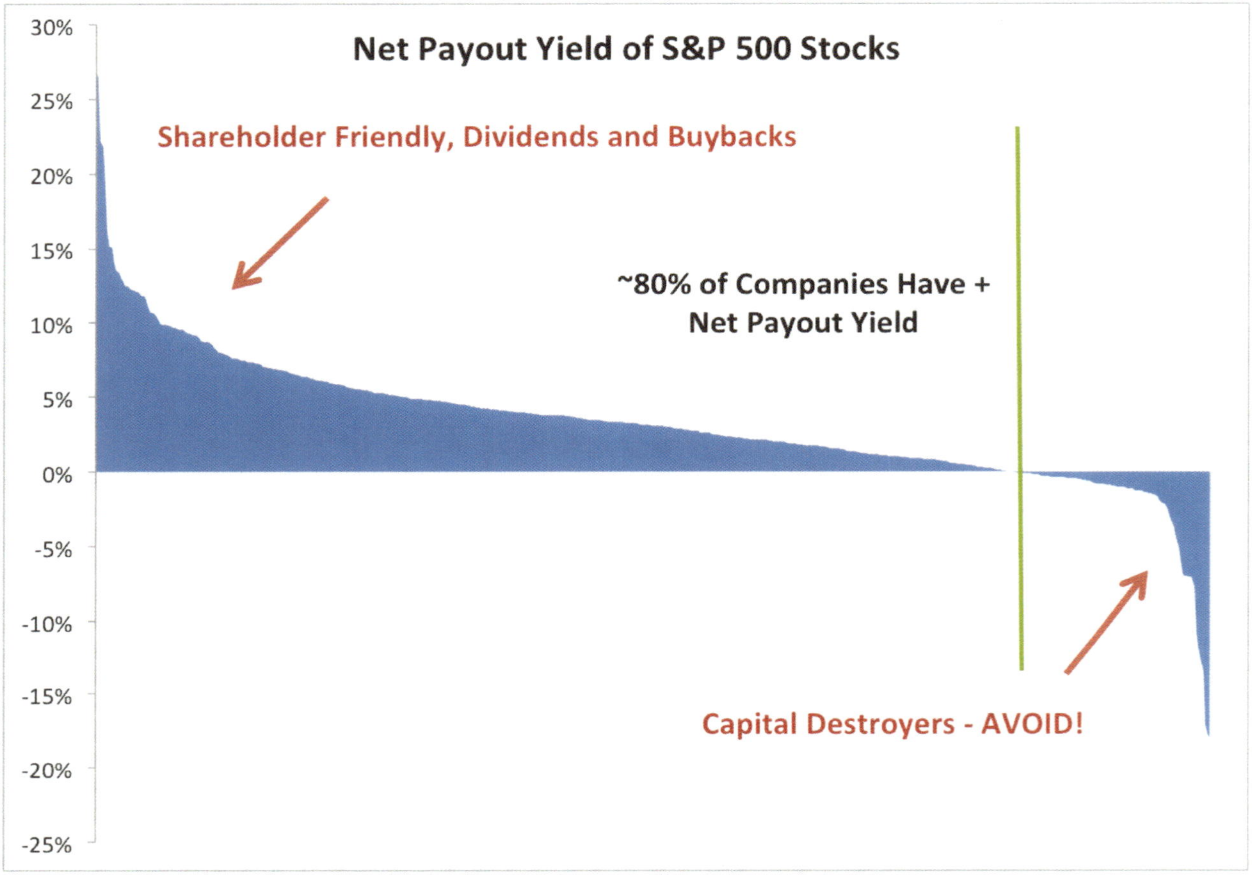

Source: Bloomberg

Another somewhat more unfamiliar method of improving the lot of the shareholder is paying down debt on the company's books. Reducing the net amount of debt on a company's books not only reduces interest costs, but also elevates shareholder claims on future cash flows. Below in Figure 17 we again find that sorting companies based on paying down their net debt results in higher returns than the broad market.

FIGURE 17 – Net Debt Paydown Yield, 1982-2011.

	S&P 500	Lowest Yield (Q1)	Highest Yield (Q4)
Return	10.96%	9.90%	13.25%
Volatility	15.57%	18.31%	15.49%
Sharpe Ratio	0.40	0.28	0.55
Max Drawdown	-50.95%	-67.61%	-46.96%

Source: Gray, Vogel, "Enhancing the Investment Performance of Yield-Based Strategies" (2012) Index returns are for illustrative purposes only. Indices are unmanaged and an investor cannot invest directly in an index. Past performance is no guarantee of future results. Index returns do not reflect any management fees, transaction costs or expenses. This example is purely hypothetical.

Do all of the measures convey the same information, or is there a benefit to combining the yield measures into one yield statistic? Below in Figure 18 we combine all three measures of returning cash to investors into one holistic yield measure that we refer to as "Shareholder Yield".

FIGURE 18 – Shareholder Yield, 1982-2011.

	S&P 500	Lowest Yield (Q1)	Highest Yield (Q4)
Return	10.96%	9.22%	15.04%
Volatility	15.57%	18.45%	15.40%
Sharpe Ratio	0.40	0.25	0.67
Max Drawdown	-50.95%	-65.96%	-47.97%

Source: Gray, Vogel, "Enhancing the Investment Performance of Yield-Based Strategies" (2012) Index returns are for illustrative purposes only. Indices are unmanaged and an investor cannot invest directly in an index. Past performance is no guarantee of future results. Index returns do not reflect any management fees, transaction costs or expenses. This example is purely hypothetical.

Combining all three measures into one factor results in a substantial increase in absolute returns. The simple shareholder yield portfolio outperformed the S&P 500 by over four percentage points a year. While a $100,000 portfolio invested in the S&P 500 in 1982 would have been worth approximately $2.3 million at the end of 2011, the portfolio investing in high shareholder yield stocks would have been worth $6.7 million.

FIGURE 19 – Various Measures of Cash Flow Yields, 1982-2011.

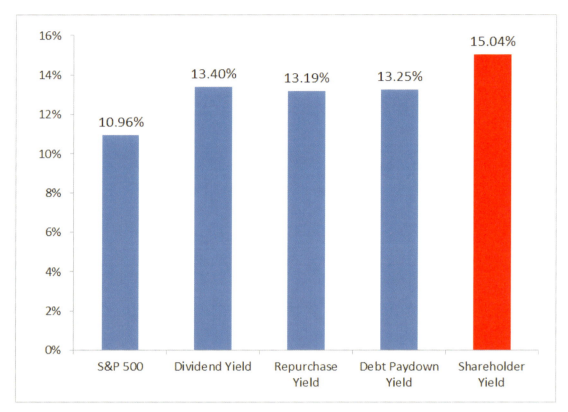

Below in Figure 20 is an equity curve depicting all three portfolios from 1982-2011 - the S&P 500, the high dividend portfolio, and the high shareholder yield portfolio. It is apparent that the valuation bubble in 2000-2003 was concentrated in the overvalued large cap stocks, and not in the dividend and shareholder yield stocks – neither of which experienced much of a decline.

FIGURE 20 — Various Measures of Cash Flow Yields, 1982-2011.

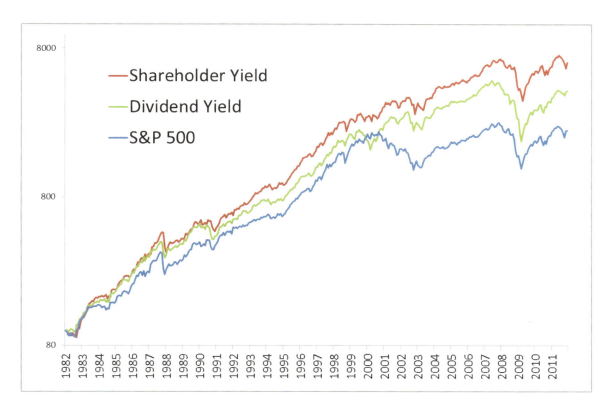

Source: Gray, Vogel, "Enhancing the Investment Performance of Yield-Based Strategies" (2012) Index returns are for illustrative purposes only. Indices are unmanaged and an investor cannot invest directly in an index. Past performance is no guarantee of future results. Index returns do not reflect any management fees, transaction costs or expenses. This example is purely hypothetical.

Figure 21 is a table of the year by year returns of the three portfolios. While the S&P 500 has experienced a "lost decade" since the turn of the new millennium with returns of only 0.54% per year, the table details the outsized performance of the dividend and shareholder yield portfolios.

FIGURE 21 — S&P 500, Dividend Portfolio, Shareholder Yield Portfolio, 1982-2011.

	S&P 500	Dividend Yield	Shareholder Yield
1982	21.48%	24.57%	23.11%
1983	22.50%	25.26%	37.78%
1984	6.15%	18.59%	15.34%
1985	31.65%	34.46%	33.50%
1986	18.60%	26.08%	24.91%
1987	5.17%	3.01%	9.70%
1988	16.61%	19.58%	17.80%
1989	31.69%	37.79%	32.82%
1990	(3.10%)	(17.36%)	(8.15%)
1991	30.47%	28.84%	28.16%
1992	7.62%	12.48%	17.60%
1993	10.08%	18.29%	21.37%
1994	1.32%	1.35%	3.35%
1995	37.58%	41.53%	44.48%
1996	22.96%	17.25%	23.51%
1997	33.36%	38.56%	34.20%
1998	28.58%	20.87%	15.43%
1999	21.04%	(9.12%)	5.19%
2000	(9.10%)	27.87%	23.16%
2001	(11.89%)	8.34%	0.88%
2002	(22.10%)	(7.11%)	(6.39%)
2003	28.68%	26.06%	31.51%
2004	10.88%	13.45%	8.54%
2005	4.91%	3.18%	5.13%
2006	15.80%	24.54%	25.73%
2007	5.49%	(5.66%)	7.36%
2008	(37.00%)	(37.36%)	(34.99%)
2009	26.46%	15.27%	31.07%
2010	15.06%	20.13%	16.27%
2011	2.01%	16.25%	1.40%
Return	10.96%	13.40%	15.04%
Volatility	15.57%	15.12%	15.40%
Sharpe Ratio	0.40	0.58	0.67
Max Drawdown	-50.95%	-61.36%	-47.97%

Source: Gray, Vogel, "Enhancing the Investment Performance of Yield-Based Strategies" (2012) Index returns are for illustrative purposes only. Indices are unmanaged and an investor cannot invest directly in an index. Past

For a longer look at combining cash flow metrics, we look to one of the most comprehensive studies on classic quantitative factor screening in the book by James O'Shaughnessy, _What Works on Wall Street_. There is a chapter on shareholder yield (but he does not include debt paydown so under our definitions it is net payout yield). He finds that high dividend yielding stocks outperformed the CRSP large stocks universe by 1.18 percentage points per year from 1928-2009, and that including net buybacks increased the returns another 1.92 percentage points per annum. (He also finds that more concentrated portfolios can add another 1-3 percentage points per annum on top of this number.)

O'Shaughnessy finds that returns for the top decile of shareholder yield stocks were positive for every decade, with the exception of the 1930s. Indeed, the *excess* returns over large stocks have been consistent and positive every decade since the 1930s. Not surprisingly, with the advent of the SEC rule 10b-18 in 1982, two of the three decades with the largest excess returns were the 1980s and 2000s. Excess returns of shareholder yield above large stocks averaged 2.37% per annum from the 1930s through the 1970s, while the excess returns averaged 4.76% per annum in the 1980s through the 2000s.

CHAPTER 5

Portfolio Characteristics

Many detractors of value and yield strategies argue that the high yield portfolios would have had higher returns only as compensation for bearing more risk. This feature has been true for the highest quartile of dividend yield stocks as they had larger drawdowns from the financial crisis of 2008-2009, but the higher drawdowns are not present in the high shareholder yield portfolio.

We ran a quick screen across the three portfolios at the end of April 2013, and Figure 22 below details common stock characteristics for each portfolio. While this is only a snapshot in time, it perhaps will be broadly instructive to see some differences between the portfolios. A factor definition list can be found in Appendix C.

First, we look at the various yields for the portfolios, market capitalization weighted. Not surprisingly, the dividend yield portfolio has a dividend yield that is over 1 percentage point above the S&P 500 and shareholder yield portfolio's dividend yield. However, the S&P 500 and dividend yield portfolios buy back very little stock. The shareholder yield portfolio, on the other hand, buys back a significant amount of stock (2.7%) as well as pays down quite a bit of debt (14.9%, though mostly due to financials deleveraging currently). These cash flow policies result in a shareholder yield portfolio that has a net payout yield of 5.1% and a shareholder yield of 20%.

FIGURE 22 —Yields for the S&P 500, Dividend Yield Portfolio, and Shareholder Yield Portfolio, April 2013.

Market Capitalization Weighted Portfolios	Dividend Yield	Net Buyback Yield	Debt Paydown Yield	Shareholder Yield
S&P 500	2.1%	0.6%	1.8%	4.6%
Top 25% Dividend Yield	3.5%	0.1%	2.2%	5.8%
Top 25% Shareholder Yield	2.4%	2.7%	14.9%	20.0%

Source: Bloomberg

Now we look at some fundamental factors that help visualize the characteristics of each portfolio. We reported the median value for each factor across each portfolio. One potential reason the dividend portfolio is often seen as risky is that the stocks often pay out a high percentage of their earnings as dividends, which may not be sustainable. If the top dividend yield portfolio is adjusted to reflect a similar payout, the yield is nearly identical to the S&P 500. Combining a high payout and high debt makes a company susceptible to cutting or eliminating their dividend in the future. In addition, the debt levels for the high dividend portfolio tend to be higher than the S&P 500 and shareholder yield portfolios.

FIGURE 23 – Median Dividend Policies and Debt, Leverage Factors for the S&P 500, Dividend Portfolio, and Shareholder Yield Portfolio, December 2012.

Median Values	Dividend Payout	Debt to Assets	Debt to Equity
S&P 500	28.08	24.00	59.66
Top 25% Dividend Yield	64.02	30.69	88.35
Top 25% Shareholder Yield	26.95	22.03	64.94

Source: Bloomberg

The shareholder yield portfolio ranks as the best portfolio across five common valuation metrics, which possibly may be one of the main drivers of the strong returns to the portfolio.

FIGURE 24 – Median Valuation Metrics for the S&P 500, Dividend Yield Portfolio, and Shareholder Yield Portfolio, December 2012.

Median Values	Price to Earnings	Price to Sales	Price to Book	Price to Free Cash Flow	EV to EBITDA
S&P 500	17.79	1.78	2.70	18.44	9.86
Top 25% Dividend Yield	16.73	1.74	2.29	17.88	9.39
Top 25% Shareholder Yield	14.13	1.48	1.90	11.22	7.39

Source: Bloomberg

We have shown that portfolios selected based on shareholder yield have outperformed both high dividend yield portfolios and market capitalization weighted indices, and it is more important than ever to have a holistic method to analyze cash distributions. In the next chapter we examine a few practical extensions to the basic screening methods we have described thus far.

CHAPTER 6

Future Extensions

There are many extensions that an investor could explore after reading this short book. We touch briefly on a few of the ideas below and leave the rest to the enterprising analyst to examine further.

Momentum and Value Filters

Long time readers know that we are proponents of using momentum and trend approaches to investing, as well as simple value factors. We have found that adding a simple momentum or value sort on a high yielding portfolio could have improved returns noticeably and consistently over time as well as reducing volatility and drawdowns.

Rerunning the same backtests as before, we sort the final shareholder yield portfolio into three groups based on six month momentum (total returns). As you can see below in Figure 25, momentum adds 1.76% in annual returns.

FIGURE 25 – Various Measures of Cash Flow Yields, 1982-2011.

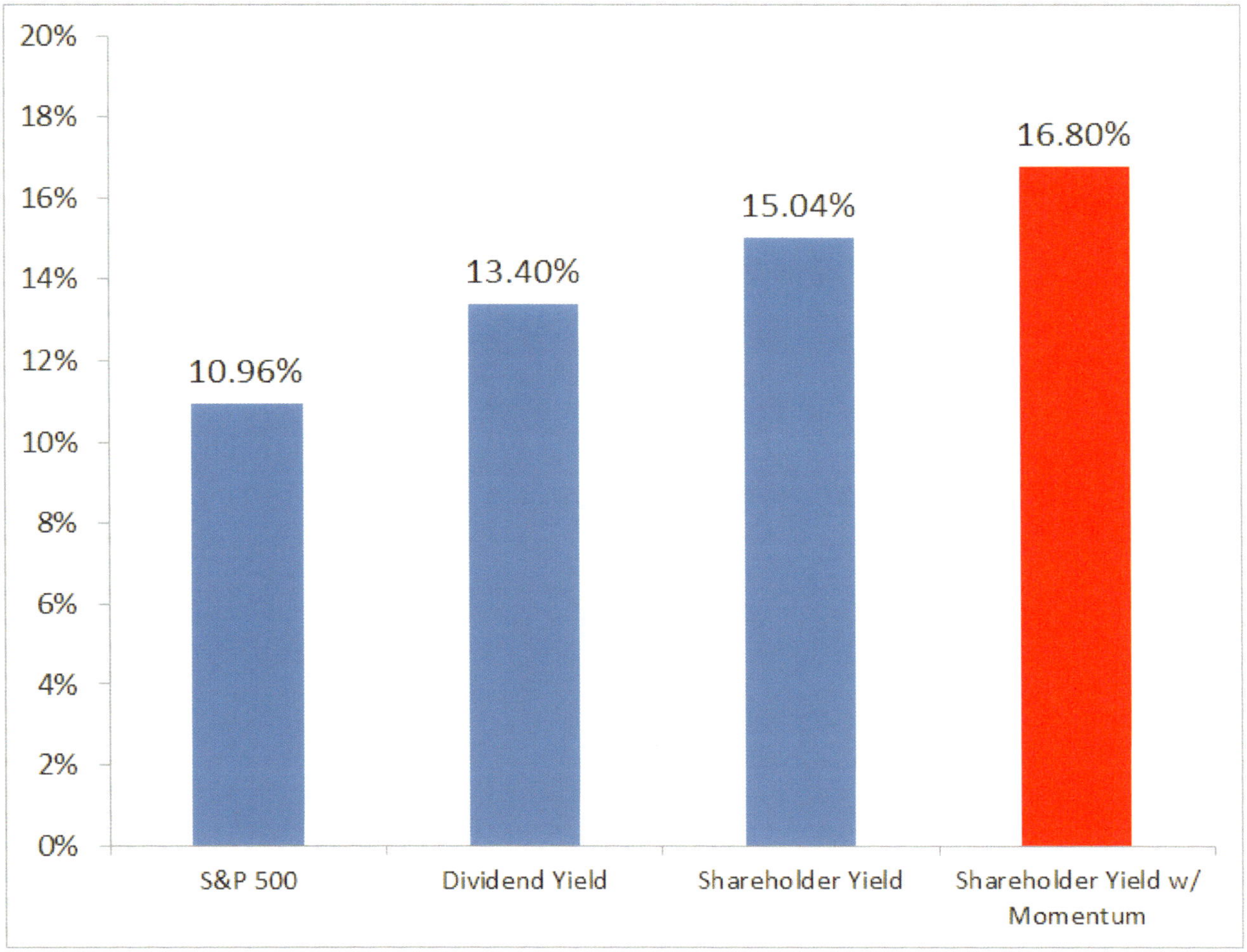

Source: Gray, Vogel, "Enhancing the Investment Performance of Yield-Based Strategies" (2012) Index returns are for illustrative purposes only. Indices are unmanaged and an investor cannot invest directly in an index. Past performance is no guarantee of future results. Index returns do not reflect any management fees, transaction costs or expenses. This example is purely hypothetical.

Payout Ratio

Often many investors cite the total amount of dividends paid out of earnings as a percentage, in the belief that companies that pay out less of the total earnings are safer and thus perform better. We believe this to be the case with dividend yield, but not so for the more holistic shareholder yield. Gray and Vogel take up this topic in their paper *"Enhancing the Investment Performance of Yield-Based Strategies" (2012).*

Dividend Policy (Initiators, Growers, Eliminators, etc.)

Many indices and portfolios categorize companies into their dividend policy and show how the stocks perform relative to their current dividend focus. While we found that dividend growers, initiators, and all dividend stocks outperformed dividend cutters, eliminators, and non-dividend paying stocks, we found that the none of the former outperformed a simple high dividend yield portfolio (and as an extension, a high shareholder yield portfolio).

Weighting Schemes

Often equal weighting portfolios results in superior risk adjusted returns. While we presented results here for value-weighted portfolios to be conservative, we have found that a simple equal weight could have added some additional returns.

Sectors

Some analysts claim it is not accurate to compare stocks from various sectors due to their particular structural differences. However, Richard Tortoriello has also presented backtests in his book *Quantitative Strategies for Achieving Alpha* (2009) that demonstrate that shareholder yield portfolios would have generated alpha in all ten US equity sectors when examined independently.

Foreign Equities

Historically, investments in high yielding dividend stocks have performed well across the globe. However, U.S. companies spend more on share buybacks as a percentage of earnings than other countries, and therefore the shareholder yield approach abroad has a less significant impact than it does domestically. The trend to more buybacks should continue as more companies embrace the tax benefits of buybacks as companies have in the US. A research piece that covers buyback and dividend investing in foreign equities is "The Importance Of Dividends And Buybacks: Ratios For Gauging Equity Values" by Jeremy Schwartz (2011).

While these are just a few extensions to the simple concept of shareholder yield, Appendix A includes a literature review with links to many more pieces on dividend investing that will provide fruitful ideas for constructing stock portfolios.

CHAPTER 7

Practical Implementation – Investing Using Shareholder Yield

For those looking to implement a shareholder yield approach to investing in equities, or to transition from a dividend only focus, there are a few resources available to the investor.

Stock Screeners

There are countless stock screening applications on the internet ranging from somewhat limited free screeners (Yahoo Finance or MarketWatch) to highly customizable professional screeners (Ned Davis or Bloomberg). There are too many websites to review here, but it is essential for the investor to do his or her homework as the screeners have various levels of quality. Some screeners allow back testing with survivorship biased databases, so caution is warranted.

There are only a few sites that have shareholder yield criteria as a preset screen that we can find. Below is a list of sites with shareholder yield as a preset factor:

- Turnkey Analyst
- Value-Investing.eu
- Ned Davis Research
- YCharts

Portfolio123, Bloodhound System, and Bloomberg have fully customizable screeners for customized solutions.

The book will have a homepage that will update with links to resources at www.shareholderyield.com.

CHAPTER 8

Summary

When faced with structural changes in a market, it is important to adjust the investment approach to take into account the changes. As John Maynard Keynes famously stated, "When the facts change, I change my mind. What do you do sir?"

It is vital to include all of the various channels that a company uses to distribute its cash flows, rather than relying on picking stocks based on dividend yields alone. Below is a short summary of the findings outlined in this paper:

- Dividends and their reinvestment contributed a major portion of the stock market total return over time.
- Portfolios that invested in high yielding dividend stocks have outperformed low yielding portfolios and broad market indices in the U.S. and in foreign markets.
- Portfolios that invested in high yielding dividend countries have outperformed low yielding countries as well as broad indices of countries.
- Dividends are only one use of a company's cash flow. Other uses include stock buybacks, debt paydown, acquisitions, and reinvestment in the company.
- Due to tax treatment, as well as structural changes in the 1980's, U.S. companies have shifted their payout mix to include more stock buybacks.
- Accounting for other ways that companies return cash to shareholders is vital to assessing a stock's attractiveness.
- Portfolios that invested in companies with high dividend yields, high net buyback yields, and high net debt paydown yields have outperformed the broad market.

- Portfolios that invested in stocks with a more holistic cash flow distribution focus, such as high shareholder yield, have experienced a higher total return than dividend yield portfolios or the broad stock market.

APPENDIX A

Literature Review

William Priest, the founder of Epoch Investment Partners, advocates the use of shareholder yield in his *book Free Cash Flow and Shareholder Yield* (2007).

While he doesn't mention any quantitative statistics in his book, a few other books incorporate backtested data. *Quantitative Strategies for Achieving Alpha* (2009), by Richard Tortoriello, examines net payout yield, although he refers to it as "dividend yield plus repurchase yield". He tests US stocks from 1988-2007 and finds that the top 20% of stocks ranked on net payout yield outperformed an equal weighted version of the S&P 500 by 3.7 percentage points per annum.

An academic paper "On the Importance of Measuring Payout Yield: Implications for Empirical Asset Pricing" (2007) also takes up net payout yield. The paper, authored by Boudoukh, Michaely, Richardson and Roberts, found that, from 1983 – 2003, the Dow returned 13.4% a year, the Dogs of the Dow (which is simply sorting by dividend yield and taking the top third of the universe) returned 16.2% a year, and sorting on net payout yield returned 19.1% a year.

The authors found that "the widely documented decline in the predictive power of dividends for excess stock returns is due largely to the omission of alternative channels by which firms distribute and receive cash from shareholders." Additionally, while dividend yield has lost its predictive ability over time, the payout yield has remained a robust indicator for excess stock return.

"Weighing the Evidence on the Relation between External Corporate Financing Activities, Accruals and Stock Returns" by Cohen and Lys (2006) examines the paper "The Relation Between Corporate Financing Activities, Analysts' Forecasts and Stock Returns" by Sloan, Bradshaw, and Richardson (2006) and finds that the accrual anomaly and the external financing anomaly are closely related anomalies.

The paper "Asset Growth and the Cross-Section of Stock Returns" by Schill, Gulen, and Cooper (2007) is even more encompassing. It basically says any decrease in total assets is good, whereas ominous signs for future stock performance include acquisitions, share issuances, borrowing, and sitting on lots of cash. Bradshaw, Richardson, and Sloan take up a similar topic in their paper "The Relation Between Corporate Financing Activities, Analysts' Forecasts and Stock Returns".

Cohen, Lys, and Zach have a chapter on Net Stock Anomalies in the book *The Handbook of Equity Market Anomalies* by Leonard Zacks.

By far the most comprehensive study is the classic quantitative factor screening book by James O'Shaughnessy. *What Works on Wall Street* (2011 edition) has a chapter on shareholder yield (but he does not include debt paydown so under our descriptions it is net payout yield). He finds that high dividend yielding stocks outperformed the CRSP large stocks universe by 1.18 percentage points per year from 1928-2009, and that including net buybacks increased the returns another 1.92 percentage points per annum. (He also finds that more concentrated portfolios can add another 1-3 percentage points per annum on top of this number.)

O'Shaughnessy finds that returns for the top decile of shareholder yield stocks were positive for every decade, with the exception of the 1930s. Indeed, the *excess* returns over large stocks have been consistent and positive every decade since the 1930s. Not surprisingly, with the advent of the SEC rule 10b-18 in 1982, two of the three decades with the largest excess returns were the 1980s and 2000s. Excess returns of shareholder yield above large stocks averaged

2.37% per annum from the 1930s through the 1970s, while the excess returns averaged 4.76% per annum in the 1980s through the 2000s.

A book on dividends and dividend growth is *The Strategic Dividend Investor* by Daniel Peris (2011). There are a considerable number of tables with historical quantitative backtests that demonstrate the outperformance of high dividend yielding stocks in the US and abroad.

Jeremy Schwartz from WisdomTree has a 2011 piece titled "The Importance of Dividends and Buybacks Ratios for Gauging Equity Values." He examines the yields on a number of companies and finds that combining the two ratios results in a more apples-to-apples comparison of yields between companies due to the different structural policies and popularity of dividends and buybacks.

APPENDIX B

Tax Rates by Year

Source: "How Tax Efficient are Equity Styles?" by Israel and Moskowitz.

Table A2: Historical Tax Rates

Tax rates by year for an investor in the 95th and 99.99th income percentile of the U.S. tax code from 1974 to 2011. Tax rates are obtained from the Federal Individual Income Tax Rates History 1913 - 2011 from the Tax Foundation in Washington, D.C. and from the Department of the Treasury, Office of Tax Analysis (November 3, 2008).

	Tax Rates by Year (99.99th Income percentile)			Tax Rates by Year (95th Income percentile)		
Year	Short-term rate (%)	Long-term rate (%)	Dividend income (%)	Short-term rate (%)	Long-term rate (%)	Dividend income (%)
1974	70.0	36.5	70.0	45.0	36.5	45.0
1975	70.0	36.5	70.0	45.0	36.5	45.0
1976	70.0	39.9	70.0	45.0	39.9	45.0
1977	70.0	39.9	70.0	45.0	39.9	45.0
1978	70.0	39.9	70.0	50.0	39.9	50.0
1979	70.0	28.0	70.0	49.0	28.0	49.0
1980	70.0	28.0	70.0	55.0	28.0	55.0
1981*	70.0	20.0	70.0	55.0	20.0	55.0
1982	50.0	20.0	50.0	50.0	20.0	50.0
1983	50.0	20.0	50.0	45.0	20.0	45.0
1984	50.0	20.0	50.0	42.0	20.0	42.0
1985	50.0	20.0	50.0	48.0	20.0	48.0
1986	50.0	20.0	50.0	48.0	20.0	48.0
1987	38.5	28.0	38.5	38.5	28.0	38.5
1988	28.0	28.0	28.0	33.0	28.0	33.0
1989	28.0	28.0	28.0	33.0	28.0	33.0
1990	28.0	28.0	28.0	33.0	28.0	33.0
1991	31.0	28.0	31.0	31.0	28.0	31.0
1992	31.0	28.0	31.0	31.0	28.0	31.0
1993	39.6	28.0	39.6	31.0	28.0	31.0
1994	39.6	28.0	39.6	31.0	28.0	31.0
1995	39.6	28.0	39.6	31.0	28.0	31.0
1996	39.6	28.0	39.6	31.0	28.0	31.0
1997*	39.6	20.0	39.6	31.0	20.0	31.0
1998	39.6	20.0	39.6	31.0	20.0	31.0
1999	39.6	20.0	39.6	31.0	20.0	31.0
2000	39.6	20.0	39.6	31.0	20.0	31.0
2001	39.1	20.0	39.1	31.0	20.0	31.0
2002	38.6	20.0	38.6	30.0	20.0	30.0
2003*	35.0	15.0	15.0	28.0	15.0	15.0
2004	35.0	15.0	15.0	28.0	15.0	15.0
2005	35.0	15.0	15.0	28.0	15.0	15.0
2006	35.0	15.0	15.0	28.0	15.0	15.0
2007	35.0	15.0	15.0	28.0	15.0	15.0
2008	35.0	15.0	15.0	28.0	15.0	15.0
2009	35.0	15.0	15.0	28.0	15.0	15.0
2010	35.0	15.0	15.0	28.0	15.0	15.0
2011	35.0	15.0	15.0	28.0	15.0	15.0

*Mid-year rate changes

APPENDIX C

Stock Factors Mentioned in the Book

Debt/Asset

Total debt divided by total assets. This is a measure of financial leverage. Stocks with a lower debt/asset ratio tend to perform better.

Debt/Equity

Total debt divided by total common equity. This is a measure of financial leverage. Stocks with a lower debt/equity ratio tend to perform better.

Dividend Payout

Annual total amount of dividends declared on the common stock divided by income.

Dividend Yield

Annual dividend divided by price. A high dividend yield indicates greater value for every unit worth of stock.

Earnings Yield

Trailing 4Q EPS (basic excluding extraordinary items) divided by price (inverse of Price/Earnings). A higher number indicates greater value for each unit of earnings, which tends to drive higher stock returns.

Enterprise Value/ EBITDA

Market value of equity plus debt (Enterprise Value) divided by earnings before interest, taxes, depreciation, and amortization (EBITDA). A lower value signifies that each unit of a stock's value is used to generate more EBITDA profits, which normally leads to higher stock returns.

Free Cash Flow Yield

Operating cash flow minus (cash dividends plus capital expenditures) divided by price (inverse of Price/Free Cash Flow). A higher number is typically a sign of undervaluation, based on the company's ability to generate cash.

Price to Book

Price divided by latest quarter book value. A lower number indicates greater value, and tends to drive higher stock returns.

Price to Sales

Price divided by 4Q sales.   A lower number indicates greater value for unit of sales, and tends to drive higher stock returns

Shareholder Yield

Trailing 12-month net stock repurchases, cash dividends, and net debt reduction divided by market cap. A higher number indicates greater shareholder value per share, which normally leads to higher stock returns.

Made in the USA
Lexington, KY
31 July 2013